INSIDE.

Published in 1994 by
Welcome Enterprises, Inc.
575 Broadway, New York, NY 10012

Distributed in the U.S. by
Stewart, Tabori & Chang, Inc.
575 Broadway, New York, NY 10012

Distributed in Canada by
General Publishing Co. Ltd.
30 Lesmill Road, Don Mills
Ontario, Canada M3B 2T6

Stine, Richard.
The world of Richard Stine /
by Richard Stine.
p. cm.
"A Welcome Book."
ISBN 1-55670-375-9
1. Stine, Richard--Themes, motives.
2. Greeting cards--United States--
Themes, motives.   3. Stine, Richard--
Philosophy.   I. Title.
NC1868.S75A4 1994
700' .92--dc20   94-12455
                              CIP

FIRST PRINTING
Printed in Japan by
Toppan Printing Company

For my Dad

ACKNOWLEDGMENTS

My wife Margaret, in particular, made a major contribution to the creation of this book. Not only did she gather the material, she also edited, sequenced, and flavored it in such a wonderful and special way. And all this was done while she continued to manage Pal Press, run our home, and attend to all the other things that I know and don't know about. Needless to say, without her brilliance, *The World of Richard Stine* would be a much lesser world.

About my father: I have dedicated this book to him because he is one of the most inspiring people I've known—a true and wonderful artist and dad. Even in his eighties, he continues to work with his hands, delight in his curiosities, and play with possibilities with as much enthusiasm as he had when he was a boy. Without being able to observe his masterful approach to all that he has done, I would have had to struggle much harder to understand what it means to work totally and sincerely from the heart.

I want to thank my dear friend Lena Tabori for inspiring this project. Without her understanding, encouragement, and persistence, the whole thing would still be in drawers and boxes and in funky, little black books with dates on their spines. She is a rare gift to the publishing world.

Also, my thanks to Hiro Clark at Welcome Enterprises for his extraordinary patience, design, and production expertise; and to Linda Sunshine at Stewart, Tabori & Chang, who helped editorially in so many important ways.

The material included in this book comes from twenty-five years of work and is composed of excerpts from letters to friends, sketchbook pages, notebook writings, and finished art, much of which was first published on notecards by Pal Press.

The ~~Art~~ World ^ of Richard Stine

A WELCOME BOOK

DISTRIBUTED BY

STEWART, TABORI & CHANG, INC.

NEW YORK

Something happened to me when I was seven years old that profoundly influenced my life. I was running through the house playing after school, running through the front room and into the far end of a long hallway. As I passed into a dimly lit part of that hall, I heard a voice that said: "The world is not what it appears to be." Startled, I stopped running, looked around, saw no one. I was alone.

After hearing the voice and pausing a moment, puzzling over what had happened, I shot off running again. But a short time later while it was still light, I took a bath, put on my pajamas, pulled an overstuffed chair in front of a big plate glass window and sat looking out over the valley of our town, feeling deeply peaceful and at the same time listening to the question turn itself over and over inside my being: If the world is not what it appears to be, what is it then?

There are so many things going on, in, around and through us, that are inexplicable to the logic of the senses. What seems to be solid and matter-of-fact is often not that at all. I am sure now that the world is not what it appears to be.

How I, a minute being in the vastness of it all, struggle to uncover my own truth, is in general what this book is about. But it is also about creativity, its fumblings, gambles, and extravagances—trying to define the problems as well as to find possible solutions. As you will see, during this process I sometimes crash and burn; but then making art for me was never just about producing pictures or writing words. For me, pictures get made and words get written only as the by-products of my fits and starts as a human being, not as an artist or writer.

Richard Stine

~~When~~ There are times when things start out in one direction - everything going just fine - Then in a matter of ~~i~~ a couple of clicks, two or three, or maybe even only one of the components of the situation changes, and its direction changes in a way that is totally and completely a surprise. ~~This~~ I'm not saying this is bad or good. It's just an observation. It's interesting about change. It's interesting how so many people are afraid of it, and yet at the core of ~~●~~ their being where all their deep desires are, exist the seeds of constant and perpetual change. Desire and change and action (movement) come as a package - all tied together Like 3 vines coming from the same root ~~of~~ — with the root being desire. In this world where everything is relative, making adjustments to make one's life better, seems to be the way it goes. Every one of these adjustments is backed by a desire. But with every adjustment we try to make to better our lives we ~~●~~ also invite change for the worse. Still, we have to try? Don't we?

Man Stretching
The Limits of
His own Mind.

When the mind speaks,
which words do you listen to -
the ones that spin endless
mischief on the surface, or
the slower deeper ones that
are always true?

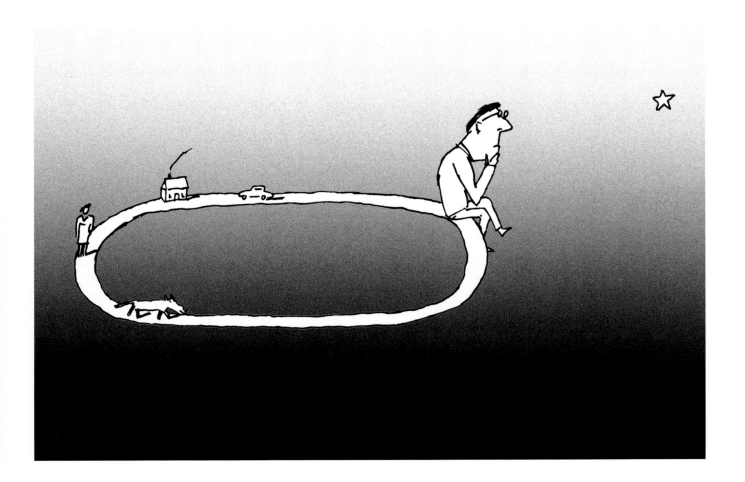

IDEAS, IDEAS, IDEAS . . . moving through my mind like subway trains—coming, going, loading, unloading, roaring, screeching, steaming, danger, electricity, tunnels, appearing, disappearing, reflections, speed, debris, noise, all rushing toward something, somewhere, alone, together they come . . . IDEAS.

IDEAS shoot up, arc, explode in sparks and fall to earth, then fizzle out in darkness again. One after another, over and below each other like lightning, bombs, broken field runners—dodging, twisting, shifting, shooting, rolling, tumbling, up and to the stars and back—high-wire acts, bubbles balanced on pointed pins, a punch to the nose, all here and gone like ghosts . . . IDEAS.

Sublime ideas are inspirational and experimental and dance on human laws. They come down naturally like falling leaves, like snow, like rain and like the shine of the sun. They are our prime movers and shakers, starting on the surface and, if they mean something, working their way inside. Following grand ideas to their conclusion takes courage.

Ideas are the bones of attitudes, and attitudes tell us how to treat the world. In return they tell the world how to treat us. Attitudes can isolate us in our hells, elevate us to our heavens, imprison us in our ignorance, or lead us to an ever-expanding understanding of life.

This world has been blind too long, its blood too red, its beat too even, its skin too thin, and its goals too gross. So where to from here? To imagination and ideas, that's where.

In the meantime a toast, to split seconds, to infinity, and to all that is unique AND the same in everyone.

i·de·a (i-dē′ə), *n.* [L. < Gr. *idea*, appearance of a thing], 1. a thought; mental conception or image; notion. 2. an opinion or belief. 3. a plan; scheme; intention. 4. a hazy perception; vague impression; inkling. 5. in *philosophy*, according to Plato, a model or archetype of which all real things are but imperfect imitations. —**i·de′a·less,** *adj.*

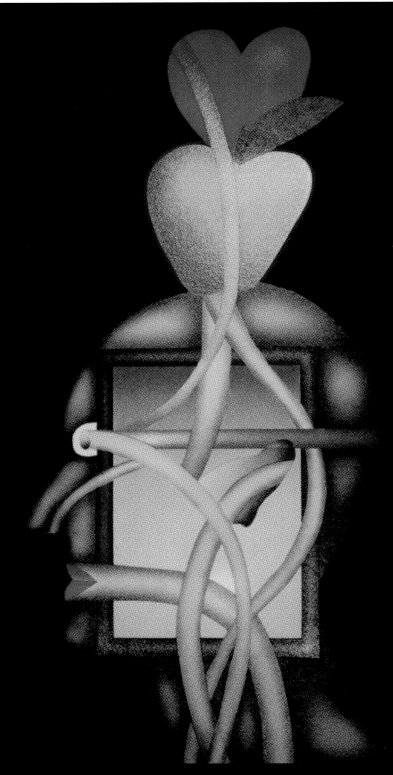

And then I think about my own thinking—how does this busy brain really work? I see two distinct levels of operation here. One is a flood of ideas that continually flows like Niagara Falls, and the other part sits in a tower like a lifeguard waiting, watching the falls for worthwhile ideas to snatch up. This way I don't have to waste time and energy shaping my art from preconceptions. I just choose from what's there and go for it, letting the hands and heart fly.

Madman attempting to empty the ocean with a spoon.

two views of ernie

Yesterday I fired up all my machines (computers, copier, scanner, etc.), got out my color markers and pencils, and dove joyfully into the sea of ideas and technology. I love my computer so much. Every time I work with it I get the feeling I can do anything, that the potential for learning is limitless. It also gives me a feeling of working in collaboration with someone rather than working on my own. In some ways it takes the edge off having to do everything right the first time. It is truly a machine of the mind. One of the best things it does is store and organize mountains of information. I store my sketchbook notes and drawings and keep coming back to them—editing, translating, twisting, working in color, in black and white, writing, nudging things this way and that. For a mind like mine, which is far too busy and too interested in too many things and is addicted to it all, it is the perfect pal.

I guess it's one of my weaknesses, or strengths—however you want to look at it—that I frequently fall in and out of love with different technologies. This probably keeps me slightly off balance (being a little uncertain of how to work with something), and away from making moves and thinking from habit.

I love the process, following the trail of clues, moving from one idea to the next. I love it so much that "finishing" something often seems beside the point.

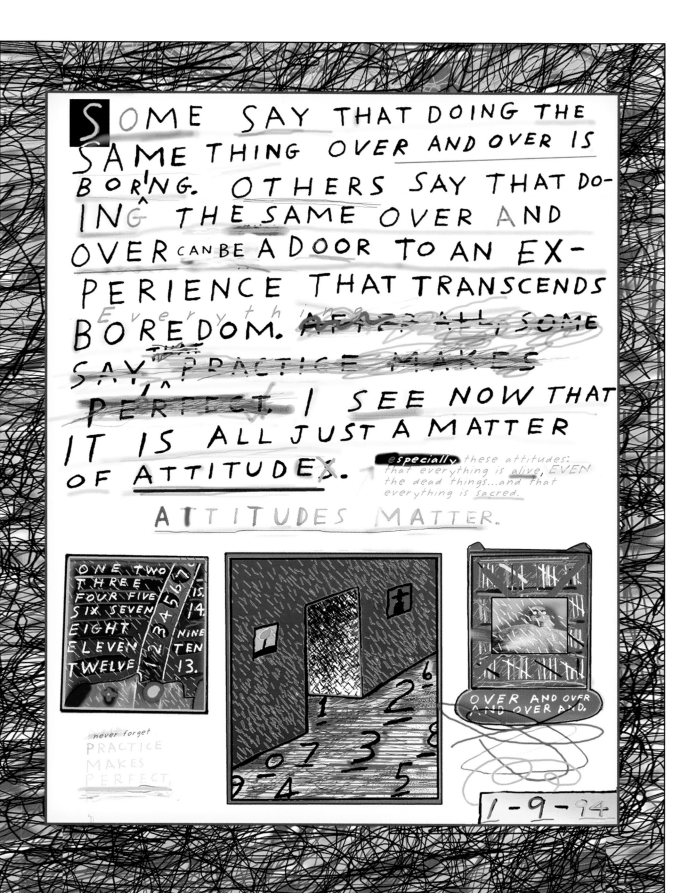

who made
the wind
and Rain?

who made
all the plants
and all the
Creatures?

who made
Time and
space?

Who made
Day and
Night?

who made
Heaven and
Hell?

who made
the earth
and all the
Shining Stars?

You Guessed it!

Mr. and Mrs. Chet Ong
in their spare time be-
tween March 3, 1936 and
April 14, 1941.

Ever wonder if Sartre had a dog?

phi·los·o·phy (fi-los′ə-fi), *n.* [*pl.* -PHIES], [< OFr. < L. < Gr.; see PHILOSOPHER], 1. a study of the processes governing thought and conduct; investigation of the principles that regulate the universe and underlie all reality. 2. the general principles of a field of knowledge: as, the *philosophy* of economics. 3. a particular system of principles for the conduct of life. 4. a study of human morals, character, etc. 5. calmness; composure.

Which came first,
The Question or
The Answer?

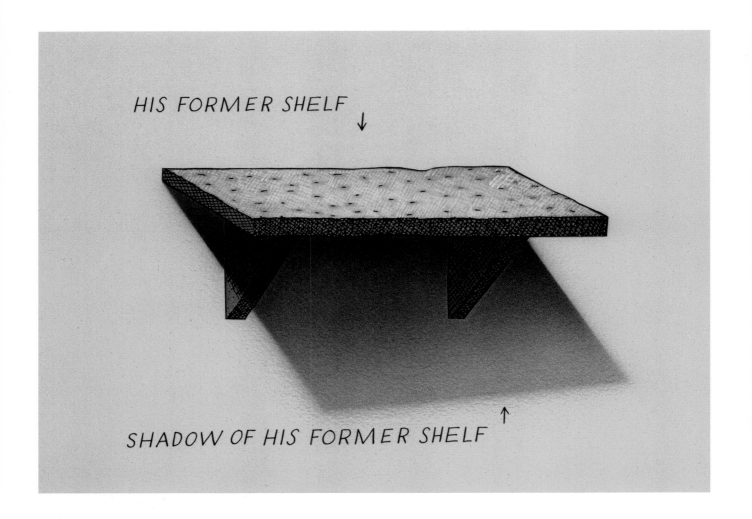

HIS FORMER SHELF ↓

SHADOW OF HIS FORMER SHELF ↑

A man once spoke
attempting a joke
Hoping to make
some Laughter.

Instead of that,
his joke went flat
and turned out a
great big disaster!

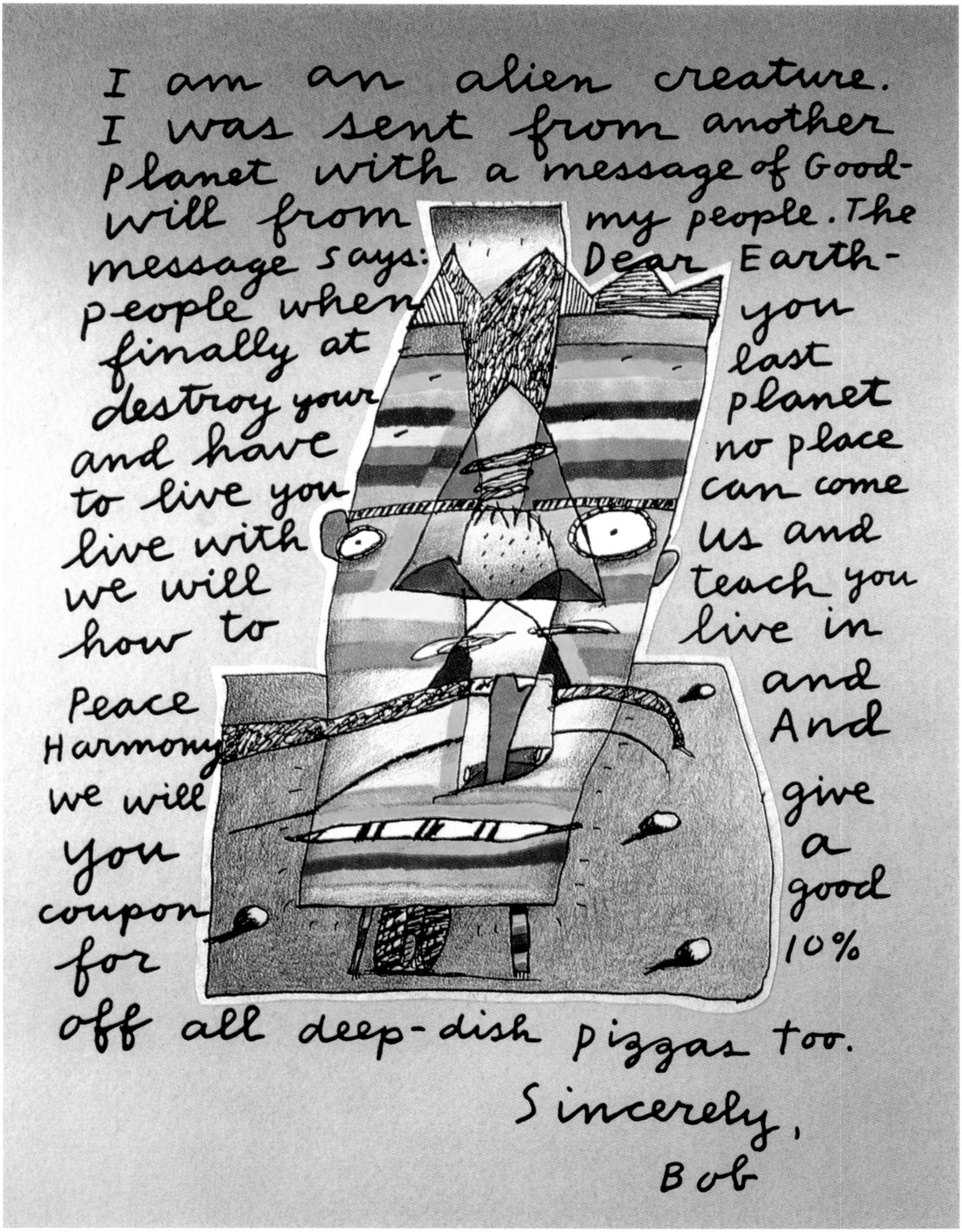

I am an alien creature. I was sent from another planet with a message of Good-will from my people. The message says: Dear Earth-people when you finally at last destroy your planet and have no place to live you can come live with us and we will teach you how to live in Peace and Harmony And we will give you a coupon for a good 10% off all deep-dish pizzas too.

Sincerely,

Bob

. . . Greta called yesterday and said there is a rumor circulating in Northern California that I died a couple of years ago, and that other people were continuing to publish my work here at Pal Press.

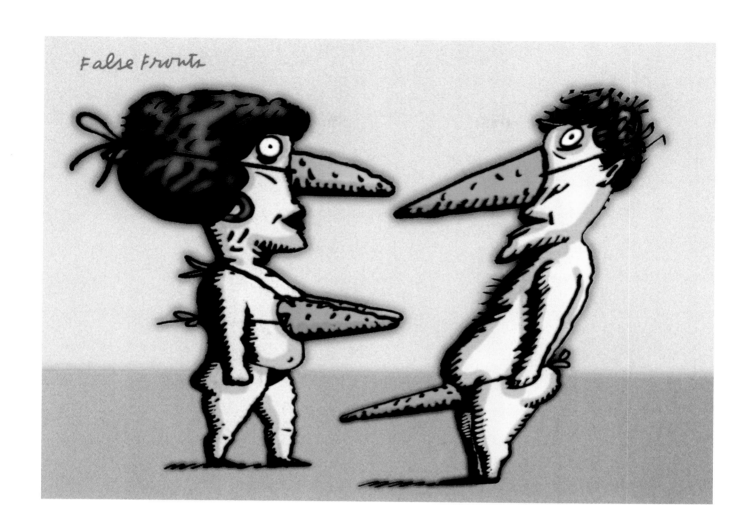

A friend once told me
that it always takes
opposing sides to
make a war. I've
never forgotten that.
If it's true, the
riddle then is this:
If you don't want wars,
how do you eliminate
opposing sides without,
at the same time,
creating another conflict?

Madmen in conflict for possession of the insignificant thing.

How do you objectify fear once you're so involved in a situation that it goes psychologically out of control?

How does one step back from the self-protection mechanism that injects complicated situations with an overabundance of emotion?

Sometimes willing yourself to be courageous through it all does not work. The emotions well up and overtake one's good intentions so much that having control never gets past being just a good idea.

My experiment right now is to attempt to lessen the emotional complications by communicating as simply as I can—to try not to feel that I have to attack or be on the defensive when I have to deal with a tough situation. Just express the truth as I see it, and then let things develop the way they will, without trying to force them one way or another.

I wonder
if one
could tell
the difference
between flying
and falling
if there
was nothing
to crash into?

Madman Spanning The Brink of Disaster By The Grace of A wonderful Ignorance.

Good Dog

Bad Dog

Sometimes, when you least expect it, LIFE gives you a big ol' sock in the nose!

Not to worry. The pain will pass, and from it you will have gained experience, which gives you information, which gives you objectivity, which gives you wisdom, which gives you truth, which gives you freedom from having to get a sock in the nose again.

Burning Question

To be ambitious, one must have desires.
To have desires, one must have needs.
To have needs, one must lack something.
Lacking something, one is incomplete.
Being incomplete, one becomes dissatisfied.
Dissatisfied, one becomes unhappy.
Unhappy, one becomes unbalanced.
Unbalanced, one becomes confused.
Confused, one's life becomes chaotic.
With one's life in chaos, one's vision becomes blurred.
And with a blurred vision, how can one live in harmony
with others, and with the earth?

So the question is: Does it always have to be this way,
or are some ambitions better than others?

What if our desires are really only
the cosmos mirroring back to us the
limits of our own understanding?
what if these desires are only indi-
cators of how far we have left to go?
What if we are in essence already "There,"
and all that we are trying to do is dig out
from underneath our ignorance of this fact?

So often we fail to remember that so many of the unrelenting (sometimes even horrific) pressures we live under, are actually pressures that our-have-ed

we selves creat- in

the first PLACE.

Cat having worked
~~real~~ very hard to get
Somewhere, now
Wondering where
it is she really got.

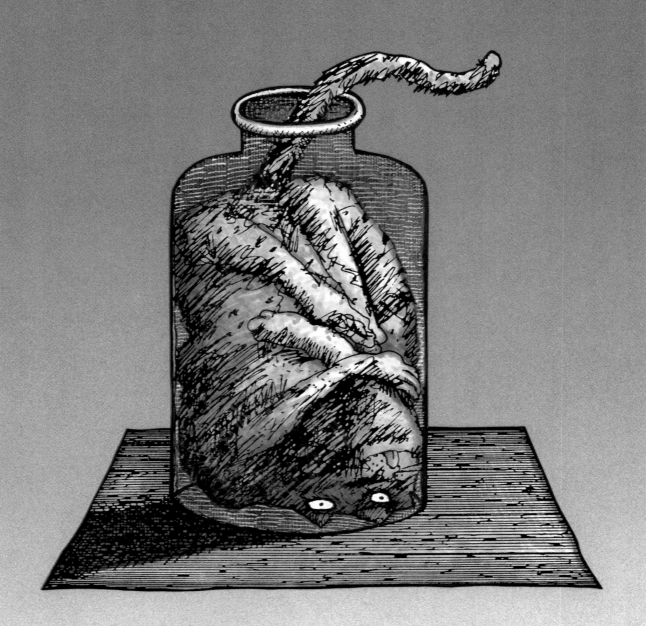

Once a man told me
m e.a.story of how he
had gone to HELL. He said
his suffering had been hideous, almost beyond be-
lief. "Describe it," I said.
He said HELL was just he
himself alone with his
lifelong accumulation of
hideous   ugly, self-
ish   thoughts
which   constantly
gnawed   on him,
inces-   santly
reminding him of his lonely
endless hopeless isolation.
THIS WAS HELL, He said.
And you Better Believe it!

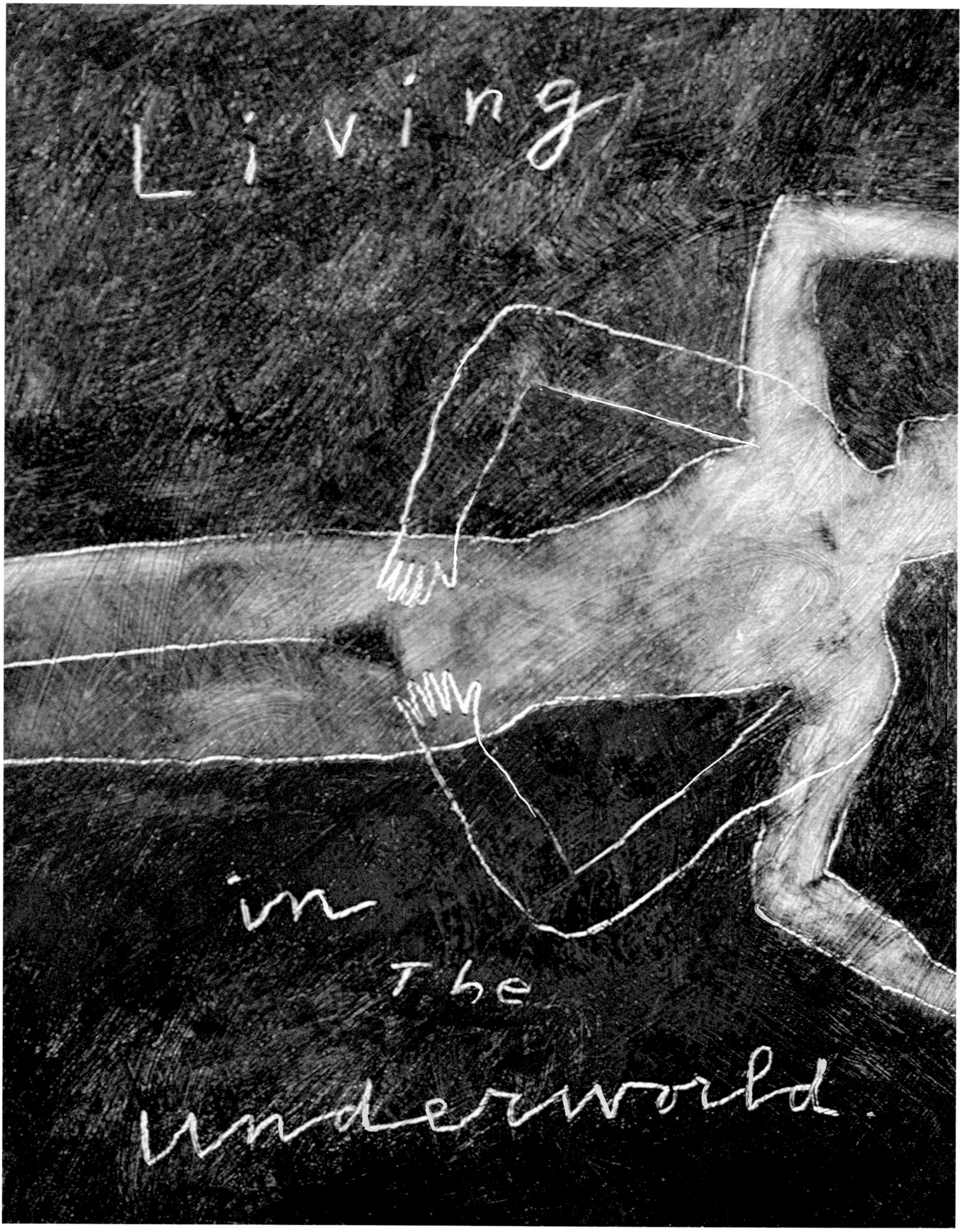
Living
in
The
Underworld.

Something in me suspects that by night
I dream I dream ⌇⌇⌇⌇ and by day
I dream I am awake.

MAP OF THE WORLD

HEAVEN

HELL

HAWAII

Our Freedom
Shrinks
when our lives
are lived
too much inside
our bones and skin
where all the fear
and hate
and need
for self-protection
are born.

THE ONLY PROBLEM WITH PEOPLE WHO THINK THEY ^HAVE A WAY OR A SOLUTION IS THAT MUCH OF THE TIME THEY TRY TO PUSH IT OFF ON OTHERS AS THE ONLY WAY OR THE ONLY SOLUTION. AND WHEN THEY ~~PUSH~~ ~~IT~~ INTENSELY, ^THEY BECOME FANATICS ~~SUCH~~ ~~IN~~ ~~FLORA~~ AND FANATICS ARE NO FUN TO BE AROUND.

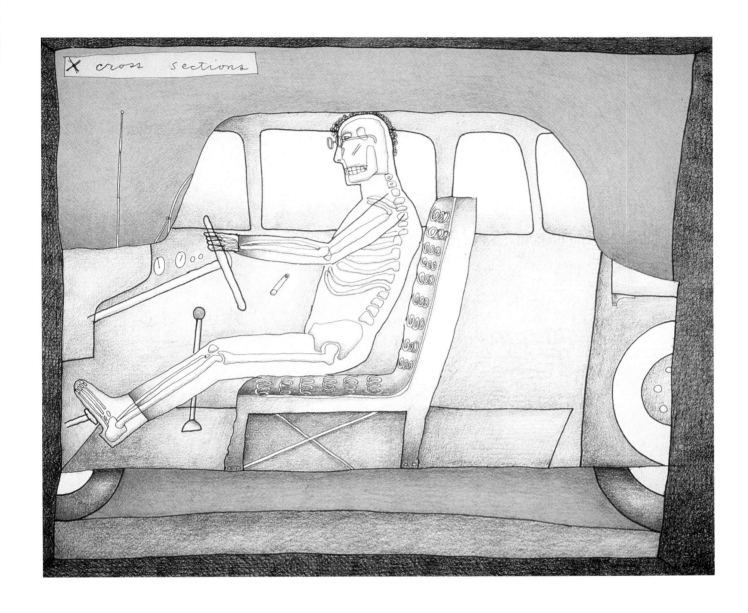

Getting To EL PASO

This guy believed with all his heart that
he knew the only way to EL PASO. He tried
hard to convince everyone that he was right.
Once he got there though he discovered a
lot of ~~other~~ people had gotten there before
him and by a thousand routes other than his.

conclusion: There's always more than one
way to get there.

The world seems to move on money—
like a living breathing ~~thing~~ moving
sea—one country to the next
talking about, thinking about,
manipulating spending, invest-
ing, printing, borrowing, steal-
ing, giving away, making,
earning, MONEY.
countries do it, states do it,
counties do it, towns ~~do it~~
and cities do it — all try to get
as much as they can.
Money talks they say.
They also say that it is the
root of all ~~evil~~ EVIL.
Everything has a price, they
say, and a penny saved is a
penny ~~~~ earned.

⊗ Money Talks

They say money talks.
That's funny, I've never
heard it say anything.
Ha Ha. Just kidding. I
know what they mean, they
mean that everything has a
price — that you could/can
buy anything if you have enough
money. Is this so? ~~Can~~ could you
buy back the Ozone Layer when
it's gone? I doubt it.
How much ~~would~~ will it take
to buy pure air or pure
water once it's all been
toxified? How many dol-
lars would it cost to make
whales plentiful again? What about
the chopped down forests — got enough
$ to put them back like they were?
I doubt it. So ~~~~ take a
deep, clean breath while you can. Look at
your children and think about it. It's
easy to see that our civilization
has a hugely warped idea of what
progress really is. And that's what's
screwing everything up. It makes me want to BARF.

What urge is there in us that
wants everything to be the same?
Fear? When things are different
and because we do not understand
why they are different, does something in us speak out, move us,
want us to shape reshape it into a
thing we can know and understand?
Why can't we leave it alone and
leave some mystery in it? Do we have to
crush it down into an understandable
little mold to be sure we have control
over it, so it doesn't run around
being different and out of control?
Out of control is scary, but isn't
it more scary to have everything
the same?

THE WORLD IS
TOO OBSESSED WITH
MAKING TRYING PROGRESS,
THAT IS TO GO ▓▓▓ FROM
POINT A to point B
PINICI
I won
about
Linear
of mo
AND
ING.

ever
Ving
DITION
DER
that
kind
vement
think-
I won-
BE

Der if it wouldnt BE
Better ▓▓▓ to never
move From point
A And to in fact to
understand that
POINT A contains all points.
Always.

Why is working hard supposed
to be such a virtue? Most everyone
struggles with insecurities of
one kind or another, or has gone
deeply into debt, making it easy to become a "hard" worker. One can
work night and day year after year
because it is "necessary" for survival.
The real virtue lies not in
working hard and constantly,
but in exercising whatever intelligence and courage it takes
to live a balanced life - some work,
some play, some rest, along with
some feeling for others and the
world outside oneself and one's
immediate friends and family.

To Work...To Work...

Home Again...Home Again.

WE ALL think we're so wide awake. That's the funny thing, maybe.

Saving for a Rainy Day

Bob and Betty were still young when they left the city and bought some hilly acreage far away, on which they built a thick-walled house, planted a garden, raised some animals, hunted, fished, and kept to themselves as much as possible. They lived far from the city because they wanted to escape the crime, pollution, traffic, noise, and people. They were tired of it all.

As you can guess, Bob and Betty were worriers. They worried about everything. But they worried most about things they saw on the news, something they watched every night over dinner.

One of those nights, they saw a panel of experts agree that in the latter part of the following year a catastrophe would happen. These experts, however, were not sure what this catastrophe would be. But they did agree that whatever it was, it would be extreme enough to affect almost everyone.

This was bad news to Bob and Betty. Even before the program was finished they decided to prepare for the worst. They would not be caught by surprise.

The very next day they started by chopping down the acres of trees around their house. They wanted enough heat and fire for cooking to last for years. They also wanted a clear view in all directions as far as they could see.

Next they laid in a supply of guns, ammunition, dried and canned food, buried their savings, and built every kind of wall and barricade they thought they might need. After months of hard work and a large outlay of money, they finished and relaxed, feeling confident and satisfied they could and would survive whatever disaster might come.

Meanwhile, it started to rain. At first it was light and pleasant. Things were dry, so rain was good. But it kept coming, turning at last into a downpour that lasted for weeks.

It was during this time, as Bob and Betty sat, safe and warm, eating dinner and watching the news, that uphill from their house a mountain of mud a hundred feet high began its downhill slide.

We go
But we
Do NOT
Know the
direction.
However
We tend
to ~~always~~
believe that
it is always forward.
Is this true
or are we
just naive?

One day, as he was driving through the city, he came to the edge of the world and fell off. His first thought, as he fell, was that all those people in olden times who believed the world was flat , might have been right after all.

Then he thought about his hopes and dreams – all the people he loved, his dog, and all the things he wanted to do.   But the fact was he was falling and falling fast – no time for thought of the future. What could he do? Then he heard a voice say: P R A Y. So he did. He prayed. He said: Dear God, if possible, please let me land in a soft place.

Cowboy, Canyon And The Horse Of Another Color

How then do we span
the distance between
what we are, and what
we want to be?

It's time to realize that absolutely everything is alive and living, even the dead things.

And it's time to realize that everything is unequivocally tied to everything else, that the world we live in is a relative world. That's a fact.

It's also time to realize that if we harm one thing, we harm all things, and that if we nurture and care for anything, we nurture and care for all things.

If we live in a relative world, and we do, why do we treat some things as if they were not a part of it?

How can we continue to be so ignorant? Is it because on the surface the universe looks so big that it doesn't matter if we cultivate limitless stupidity and make infinite mistakes?

Well, friends, trust me, it's not THAT big.

What do you think? Do you think you come
from nowhere, then after a few years
vanish back into nothing, with a few
pleasures and pains sandwiched
in between?

TRACKING BACK thru TIME (and space) I have discovered something. Let's see, How can I put it into words. Or pictures. The heart is at the center of everything, even the bad stuff. O-I don't mean the soft HEART, sweet heart, particularly gentle heart — even though that's there too. I mean a HEART that's much BIGGER THan BAD and GOOD. MUCH. I mean a HEART That has every- thing, Every L AST THing in it. A HEART THAT CONTAINS The whole universe down to the last IOTA.

(any body know what an IOTA is?) Good name for a dog don't you think? The HEART I'm thinking about even though it contains everything is still inside each of us — so in some ways it's very BIG and in other ways it's small enough to be in us. But then that raises yet another question which is: HOW big OR SMALL are we? If we are small, how can we contain a heaRT That's large enough to contain the universe. FACT is - we - NoBody is small, NoT ONE single ittibitti little human being. NOT ONE, PERIOD.

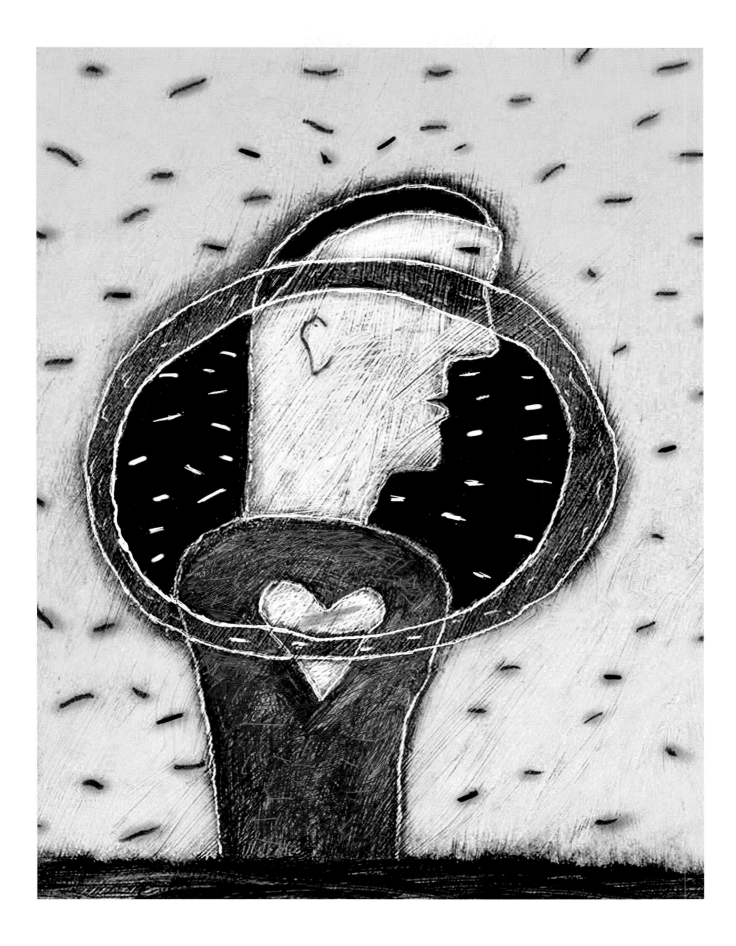

It's when you get older and the
tables turn a little that you realize
that getting and giving love come
as a package - That finding someone
to love is as important as finding
someone to love you.

I look around and see so many
people wanting to be loved, waiting
to be loved, waiting for some Big,
generous, comforting, nourishing
being to drop out of the blue into
their lives and give them ~~some~~
LOVE.   Love with a Capital EL.
The question is: Will it ever happen?
or will it ever happen the way they
want it to happen? Can it really happen that way?..... Maybe, maybe.

What is the difference between Love and Desire?

Desire wants to GET... Love wants to GIVE.

What is it in someone
that attracts us to them?
What is it in someone that
repels us? Sometimes you can
know when you first meet someone
that something about them
is special for you. Maybe you
don't know exactly what it is
then, but you sense deep inside, without a doubt, that it's
there. And instead of becoming
anxious to know exactly
what it is, you become extra-
ordinarily patient, and willing to wait however long it might
take for the magic to define itself.

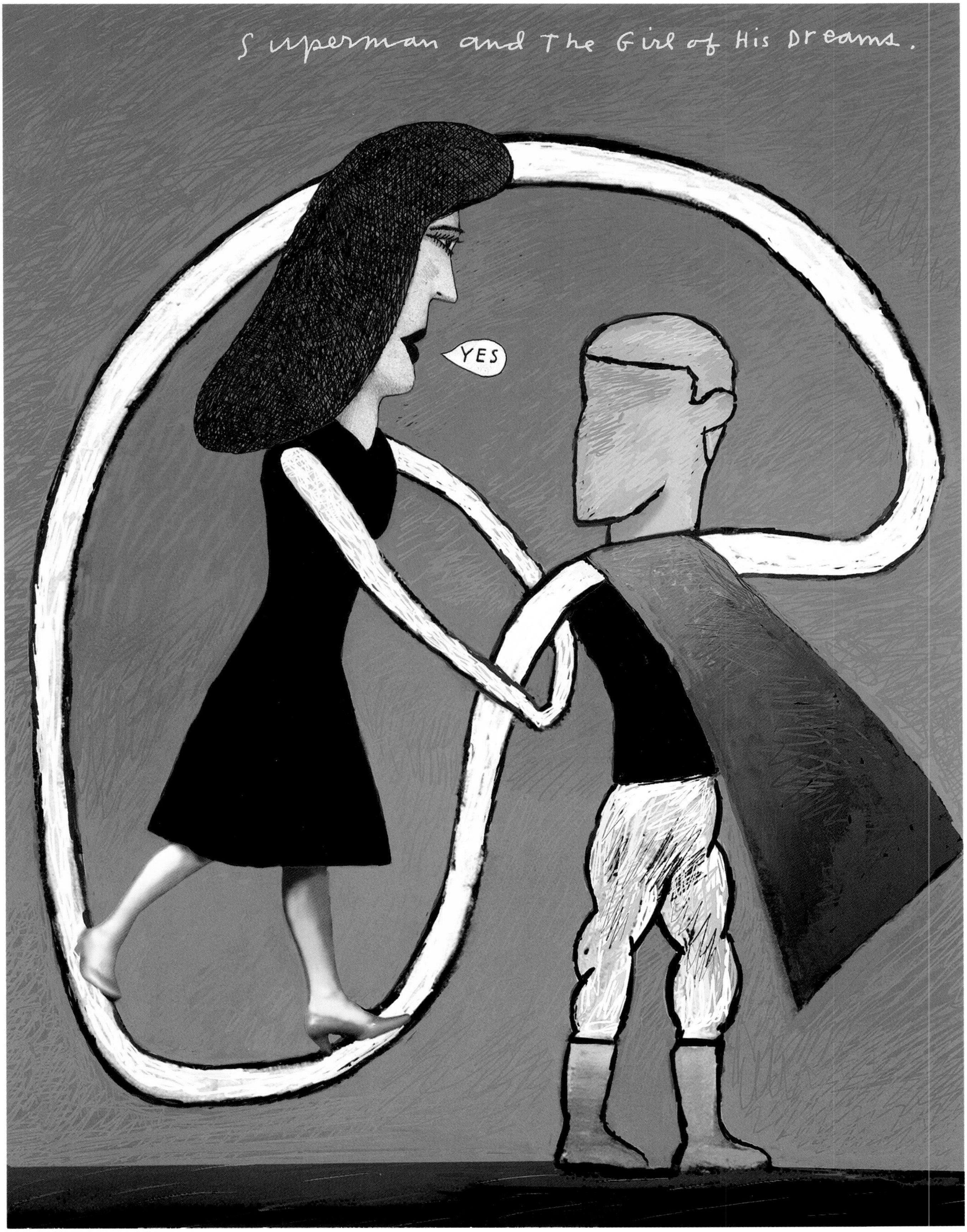
Superman and The Girl of His Dreams.
YES

Exchange of A Deep Level Affection.

Our days together
are numbered,
Infinite.

Often, when we make an effort to find the Bigger, Grander things in life, we are won-

derfully surprised by the discovery of other equally significant things along the way.

    . . . We'll get to the place where everything is so subtle the air is enough sustenance and the gods will spoon-feed us from the lower planes, and your place will be a sea of light and I'll be in there floating quietly on a gold-leafed inner tube, lying in the waves of your soul. And you are welcome to do the same in me if you want, because our universe is one. Deep down everyone knows everything lives and breathes in the same being. The mind will protest, but never the heart. The heart always says, "Together, we are all together." The mind stands back and looks and thinks and says, "This is good, that is not good." Maybe there is a time and place for that, but the heart at its core stays even. Bad, good, different, same, up, down—all exist in the mind, not the heart. And if the mind sits on the heart then it will have a nice perspective. If not, it just chases its own tail until it's kissed by an angel, the kiss of peace, and then it will never be the same. The heart will expand and explode with joy, paling the mind to insignificance in the volcano of fire and life.

In the course of our lives
things come and go – some
pleasure, some pain, some
work, some play, some dreams.
And by these things we learn
to make the heart an ocean,
and on that to go beyond the
troubles of this world.

To cleanse the Heart...

To unlock the Lock...

To open the Door...

To Live at last.

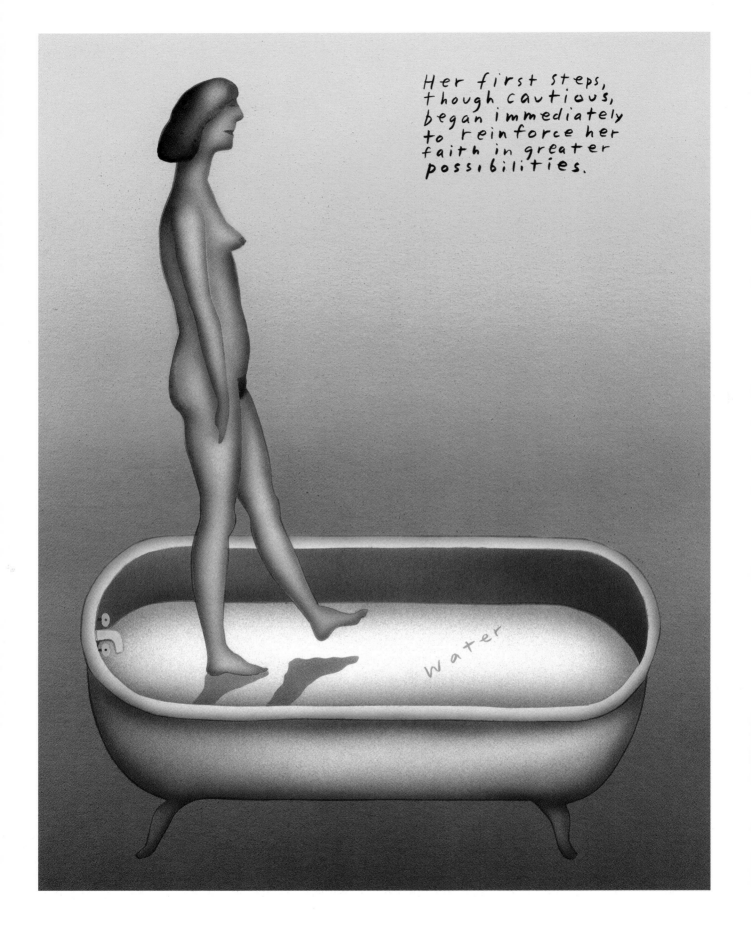

She lived without much
thought for the future.
She made do with what
she had, enjoyed her
friends, and always lived

a   notch
or   two
this   side
of   too
much   hope.
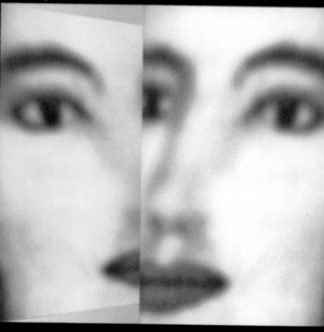
Those   who
knew   her
would   describe   her
as happy more than not,
but because her interests
were moderate in a
world gone mad with
desire, they for the
most part, considered
her strangely out of
step with reality.

Evolution

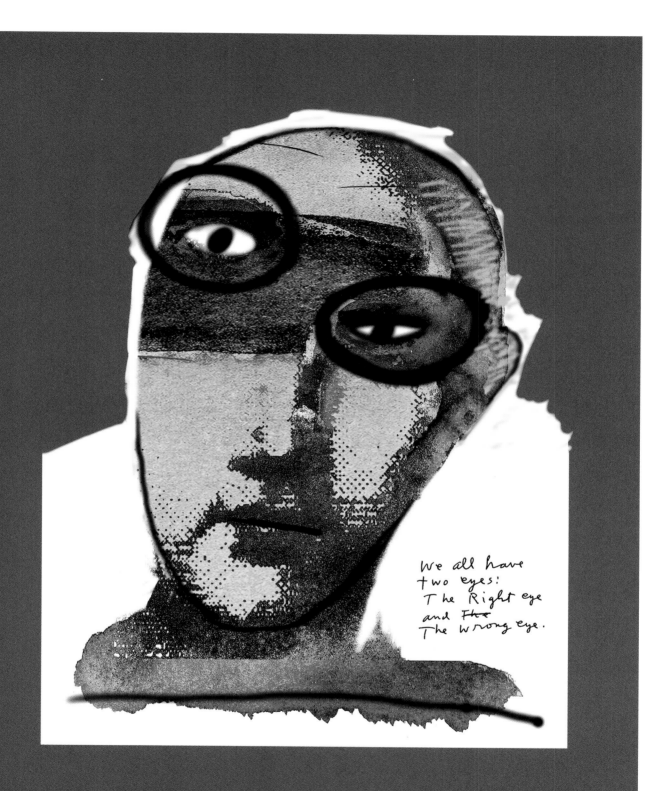

We all have
two eyes:
The Right eye
and ~~the~~
The wrong eye.

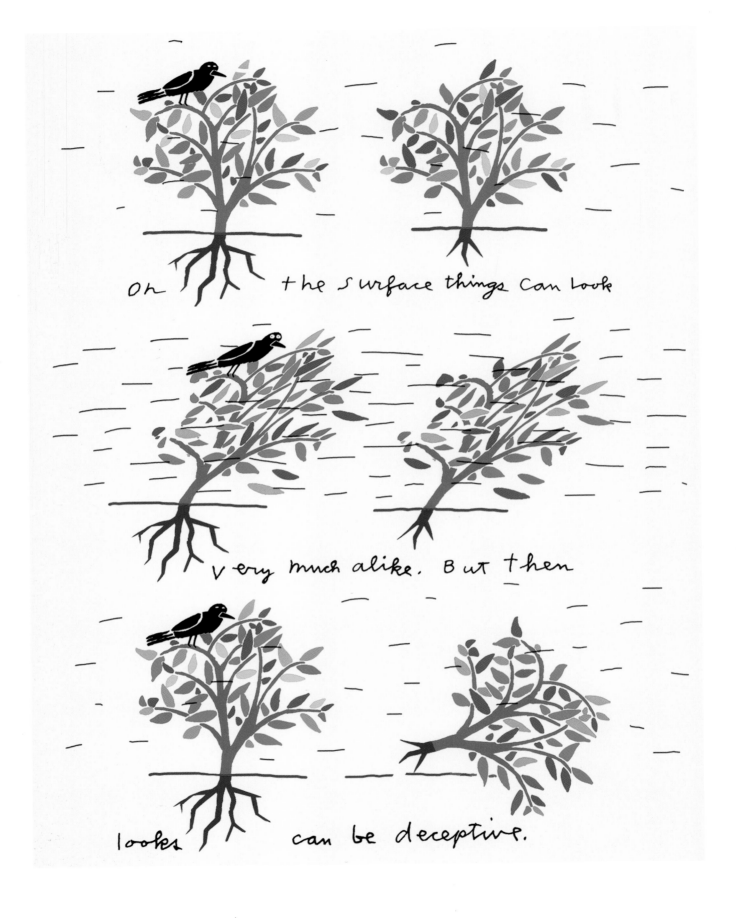

On the surface things can look very much alike. But then looks can be deceptive.

It is not
so much
what one
looks at,
as much as
what one
sees When
one is
looking.

Reaching Through The <u>Gross</u>
To Grasp The Secret of Beauty

Creativity and money are an impossible combination, like oil and water, or honest lies. How do you put a price on something unique? What is the measure of it? If scarcity is that measure, then creativity automatically becomes more valuable than gold, because after all there's plenty of gold. This isn't the way it's perceived, however, and really, if it were it would be an unworkable situation. Our prevailing attitude demands that everything has a price. The world's wheels turn on money, everything gets bought and sold. The panhandlers panhandle, we try to sell our art. We're all busy trying to get enough, or more than enough, to live on.

The getting of money takes up a good portion of most people's minds and time. When I'm not making art, I know it takes up a large amount of space in my head. And when I listen to people talk, they talk a lot about the success and failure of getting money. It seems to be necessary, but it's the other times, the times when we are not thinking about money, that really interest me.

...still you know you have
to start somewhere, and
asking a question is as
good a place to begin as
any - even if you know
that silence, ~~then~~ for
now, is absolutely all
that you will hear.

What do you think?

(From a letter to Don)

   . . . I've been thinking about giving you this book for years—*The Gospel of Ramakrishna*. To put it simply, this is a book that is not a book. It is for me pure MAGIC, and I mean that in the truest sense of the word. And since we're all interested in finding any doors to other worlds that we can, this is one of those . . . in fact, it's the best door I've ever found, at least in this form.

   It's brimming over with wonderful ideas, with encouragement, with generosity, and at the same time it puts a grand perspective on everything, besides leaving plenty of room for creativity. Every time I read it, it changes like a chameleon, turning into something different, something more. Reading it is like being in an alchemist's hideaway, where the recipes for turning dross into gold are being revealed. It is not like any other reading for me . . . it lives. The words and pages blur into something living, breathing. I'm there. Maybe this is the magic part. I don't know.

   It's like the best teacher and the best pal rolled into one. It's had a profound influence on my art, my life, my every breath. And this is no exaggeration.

   What are friends for, if not to share whatever doors they find along the way?

Zen Cat Rides A Rainbow Over The Rough Edges of The World

Miracles ⌄Indicated by the Commonplace.
Being

Hill

Mountain

Cloud

Star

Coffee

Jar

Light Bulb

Wheel

Chair

Woman

Man

Bird

Fact is: Everything is one thing!
The direct perception of
this truth is the only real
Freedom.
To get this perception,
everything and anything that
creates a division, in
which the whole is
reduced to smaller parts,
must somehow be erased.
Learning to love seems like
a good place to start.

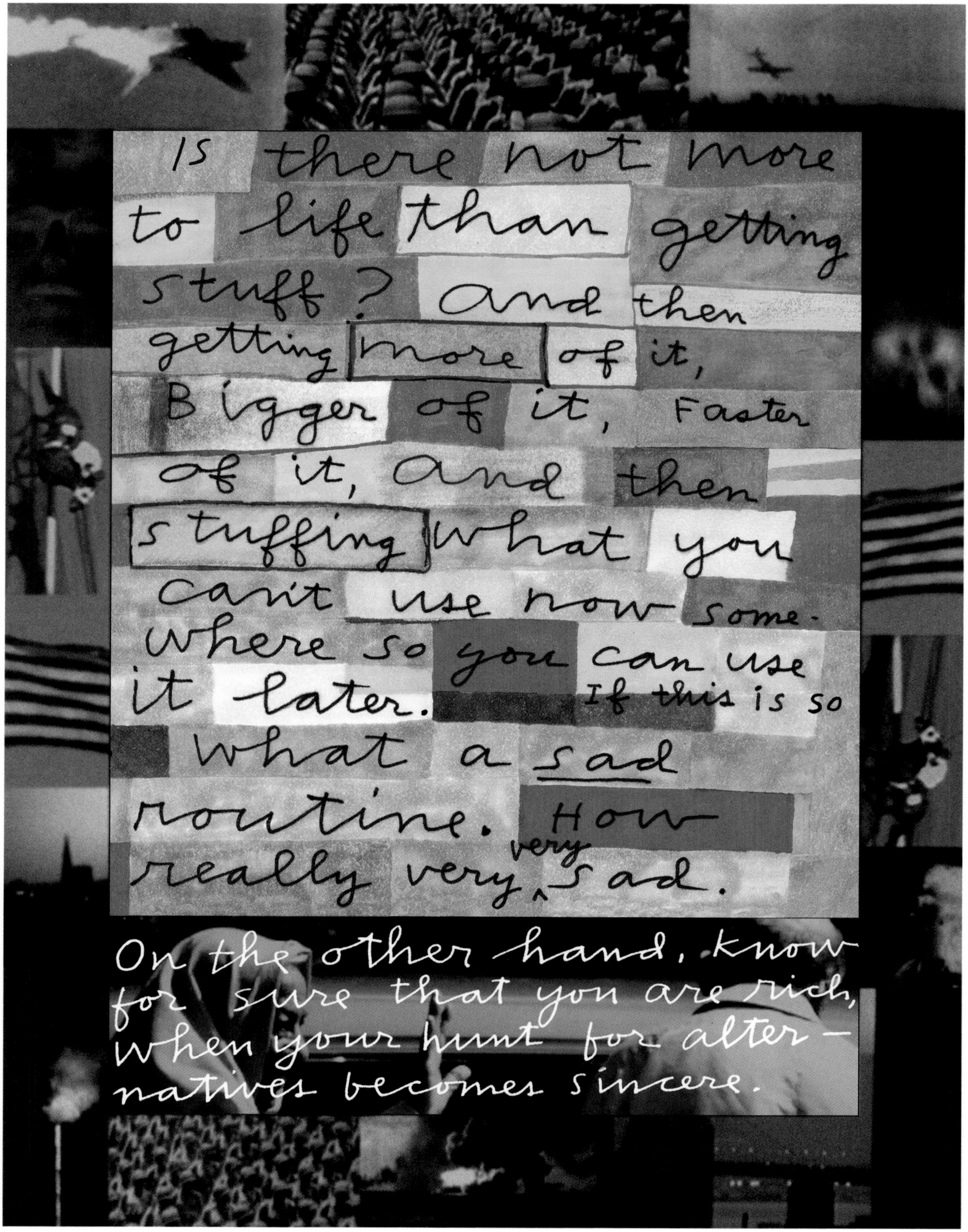

Is there not more
to life than getting
stuff? And then
getting more of it,
Bigger of it, Faster
of it, And then
stuffing what you
can't use now some-
where so you can use
it later. If this is so
what a sad
routine. How
really very very sad.

On the other hand, know
for sure that you are rich,
when your hunt for alter-
natives becomes sincere.

How will you know
when **you** have enough?
HOW WILL YOU KNOW?
When → you ← have
ENOUGH?

how	will

y_o_u   know
you   know
you   know

people are trained
by people who are trained
by people who are trained
by people who are trained
to always want MORE
AND BETTER AND BIGGER!
What a shame.
who questions all of this? WHO?

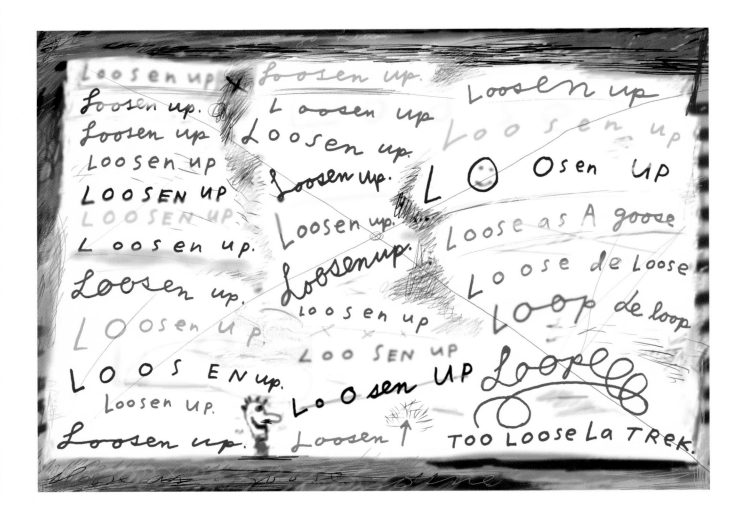

I've always loved graffiti, the straightforwardness of it, even if its subject matter is narrow and gross. Its directness has always thrilled me—impulse to image with no barriers in between, especially those imposed by an "education."

It's odd how much time we spent in school being taught, only to find out that over the years we have to get rid of, or at least heavily modify, most of what we learned there.

This is one of the great things about art and artists, especially good ones—they exude attitudes that encourage new ways of seeing and doing (the living of one's life outside of "art" especially). The great ones say to me that it's okay to think and do things that I haven't been permitted to do before. They break down barriers and reduce our limitations instead of giving us more. Whom we choose to admire is entirely personal. I mean the creative people I admire won't always be the ones you will admire, simply because our needs are different.

I want any idea I express in my art to be like a mental tattoo. Whether people like it or not isn't the question. I want it to be like the tar baby—you punch it and your hand sticks. Then you try to push away and your other hand sticks. And you keep trying to free yourself and pretty soon everything's stuck—feet, arms, legs, head, heart and so on. And there you are, helpless. And the tar baby just grins.

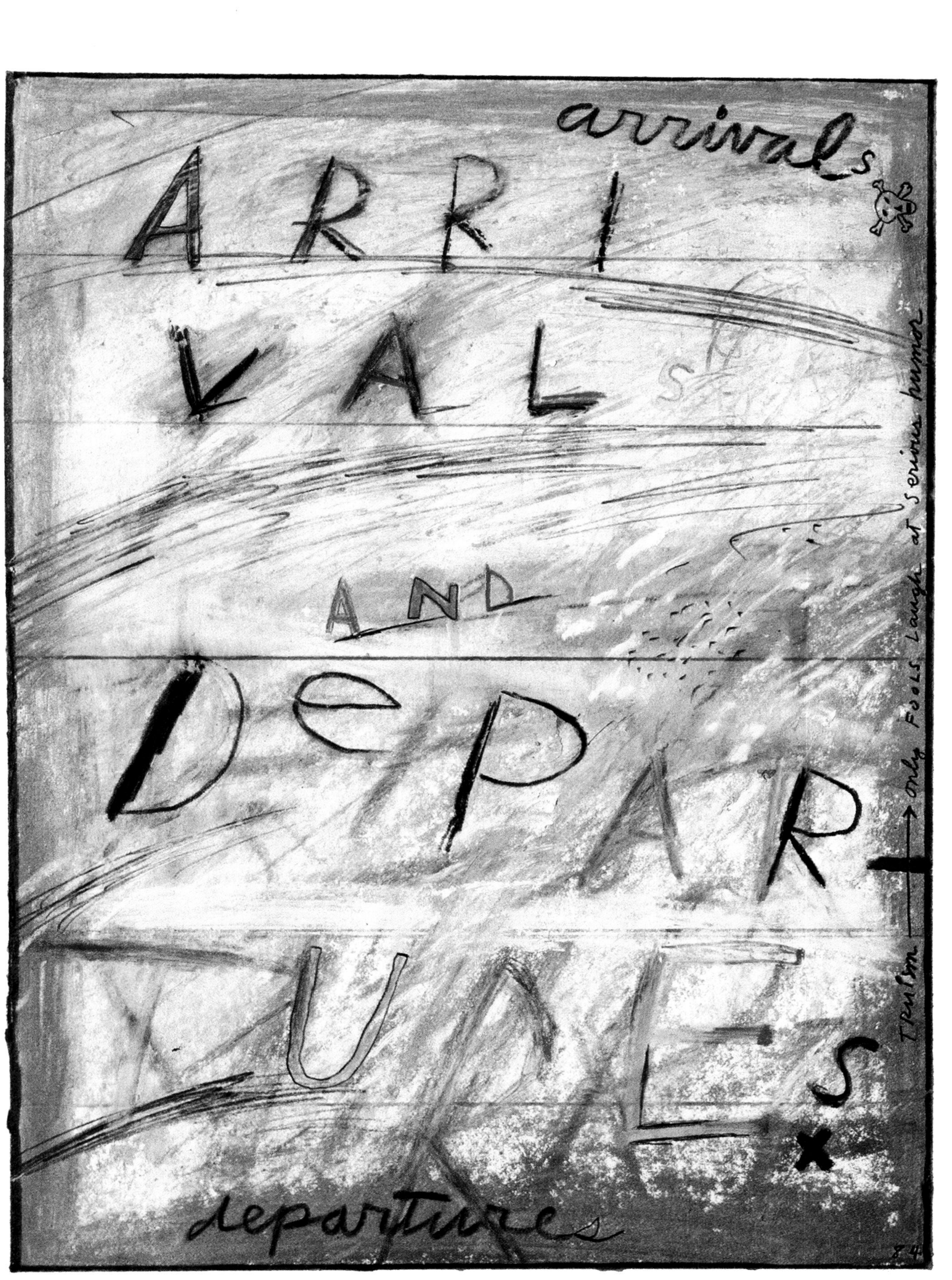
arrivals
ARRI
VALS
AND
DEPAR
TURES
departures
Truism → only FOOLS Laugh at serious humor
84

Q. What happens when you live too far in the future and too much in the past?

A. You miss out on the present!

How many times must
we go over the same
road until we recognize
that it is the same road
that we have gone over
so many times before?

Endless X progress
Endless Progress!
The changing of the
face of things,
At first one thing
quite natural And second
some cramped QUAR-
Ter Sheltering with-
OUT Grace A Body
And Mind Struggling
in Bewilderment To un-
derstand its wretched
circumstances. For
What?
Ah, the JOY of sit-
TING IN The DARK.

To tell you the truth I have a little voice in me that tells me what to do, what color to use, what pencil to pick up, what buttons to push. And as long as I listen to that voice I'm happy, even if the work I'm doing ends up in the trash, which it does lots of the time.

Sometimes the voice is not there, but I don't worry much, I work anyway. Then somehow it comes back, and I go bursting out again. It's happened this way since high school, when I did a little gouache painting of a guitar that felt as if it came through me, instead of from me. That was such a wonderful experience, and one of the reasons why I've been so enthusiastic to be a maker of things ever since. It's also why I romp through so many techniques and media—always waiting for the thrill of "it" to happen again.

Listening to that voice is more important to me than money any day. I've come close to dying (at least that's the way it felt), when circumstances squelched it in me for a time. Then when the voice finally came back, I promised myself to do everything I could, not to let anything get in the way of hearing it again.

I say voice, but maybe that's not what it really is. Sometimes it sounds like a voice, but it also sounds like me talking to myself. Maybe it's my muse—anyway, what people call a muse. I hesitate to say it's like something big using me as a tool, because that sounds so otherworldly. But then perhaps it is . . . I can't tell you for sure. All I know is that I'm happy when I'm in tune with it and miserable when I'm not.

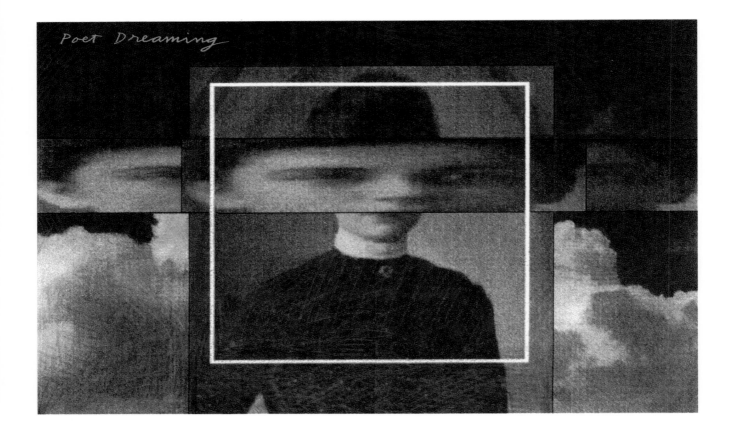

Poet Dreaming

I think the next phase of my life is going to be the poet phase. Prose I am not comfortable with, especially long, sustained stuff that's trying to make a point point-blank. I'm much more at home with feelings and imagery that come at things in odd ways. In fact, I rarely need more than a page to say what I have to say about anything. Sometimes not even that much. I want very much to try putting a book together of single-page ideas—magic, metaphysics, metaphor, and poems.

I've developed my way mostly because of my own limitations, which is why the work looks the way it does. I've simply brought it up out of nowhere without knowing how anyone else does this sort of thing. If I were a bolder type, I would probably be quite an earth shaker, real rebellious blood-and-guts stuff. But I'm not. I'm fairly timid, in fact. I do what I do because I have no choice—I need to express myself. It seems to me anyway, that I move so slowly and cautiously, that I could have been here, where I am now, years ago, if I had had just a drop more courage. But then, IT IS SIMPLE, right? I'm here now, and that's all that counts.

IT IS SIMPLE...

WE ARE WHERE WE
SHOULD BE, DOING
WHAT WE SHOULD BE
DOING. OTHERWISE
WE WOULD BE SOMEWHERE
ELSE, DOING SOMETHING ELSE.

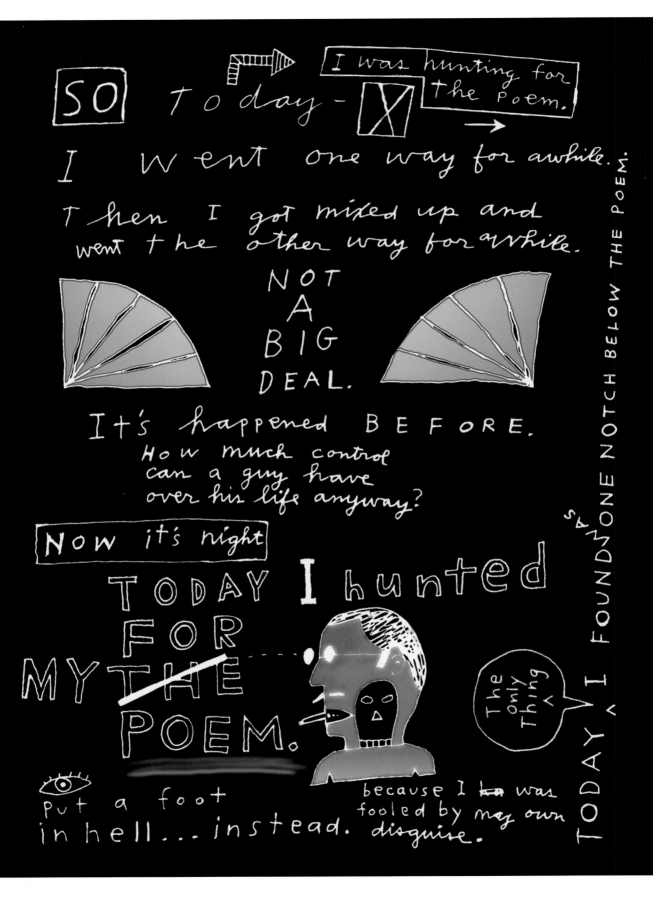

Sorting and Sorting,
I feel like Some Kind
of idea clerk: One for
this box, One for That,
and So On. My ideas
need Zip codes, maybe
even a bulk mailing rate.

... A moment later
crowds across the sun
a putting motor by,
by tiny waves, a whisper,
whispers secrets to the sky.

Down the curving distance
flutter sailings on a chilly moon,
Butterflies, and kings, and Queens
all dancers on a spoon.

In a mirror
I Look to see
what is
exactly me.
Instead I see
the sea
that is
my destiny.

What We see
Are the countless
Faucets.
Who looks for
the Ocean that
the supplies
the faucets
with water?
What purpose are
the faucets without
their water supply?

Better to
see The Ocean
than the countless
Faucets.

THE WAY IT FEELS
SOMETIMES

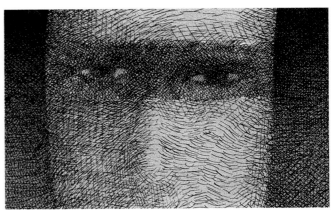

Sometimes my eyes speak better than my words.

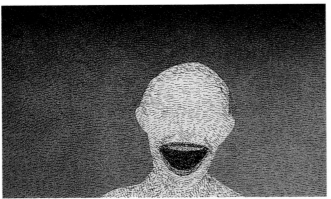

Sometimes I laugh to hide the tears

Sometimes when I move too fast I lose my center

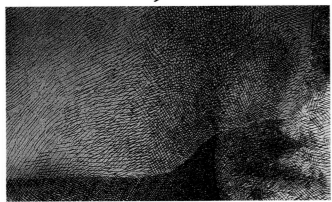

Sometimes when I look my vision is not clear.

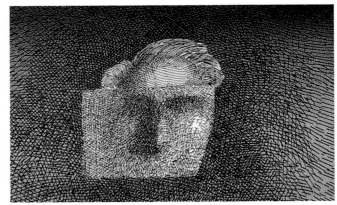

Sometimes when I think too much my feelings cannot speak.

Sometimes when I'm here I wonder why I'm not there too.

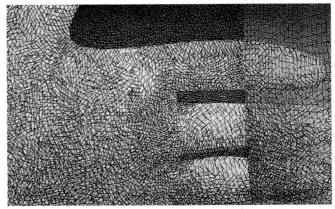

Sometimes I feel the mystery, sometimes I don't.

IF you hold something too tight, it will shatter.

IF you hold something too loose, it will drop and break.

But if you hold something just right — not too tight, and not too loose

... ah, well, you figure it out.

That the heart beats
once is astounding.
That it beats a
lifetime is miraculous.
To me its unthinkable –
like a walk to the
sun. I think it anyway...

How does one get <u>wisdom</u>? what is it anyway? I'll have to think about it. Umm. Umm. umm. Let's ◉ ◉ see. AHHHH.

ONE PART of or of be- knowing sequences tions well to choose whether guess this some self power too. How one's choices choice one makes contrary to which is circumstance a wise person's

Wisdom is difficult to define. I'm sure in many ways we are all wise. I'm also sure that in most ways we are NOT.

of wisdom ing wise, is the con- of ac- certain enough to be able or hot to do them. would imply having control and will could one implement especially if any happens to run one's impulses, not an uncommon or occurrence in Life (I would guess).

Wisdom is a kind of maturity
Being old is not a prerequisite
For being wise. No way. I know many young people who are very wise... I know plenty of unwise ones too FOR that matter. for that matter.

(Wisdom depends so much on the kind of ex- (HAVING) perience One has and also the kind of mind bent one has. Without the kind of mind that absorbs the essence of one's experience, one goes on and on doing many thing one should not be doing.

If I threw a stone

it could damage your Eye.

If I threw a stone

it could break your Heart.

If I threw a stone

it could shatter your Dreams.

Instead, I will gather the stones and build you a path over

the mountains to the ocean on the other side.

Where do you live?
In the universe?
on this planet?
In your country?
In your state?
In your county?
In your city?
In your block?
In your house?
In your body?
In your heart?
Where?

Four Thoughts I Had Today: That the eye can only see itself in a mirror... That flying on small planes is not that bad... That it only takes one spark to start a forest fire... And that sometimes the difference between success or failure, depends on whether or not we get or give a little encouragement.

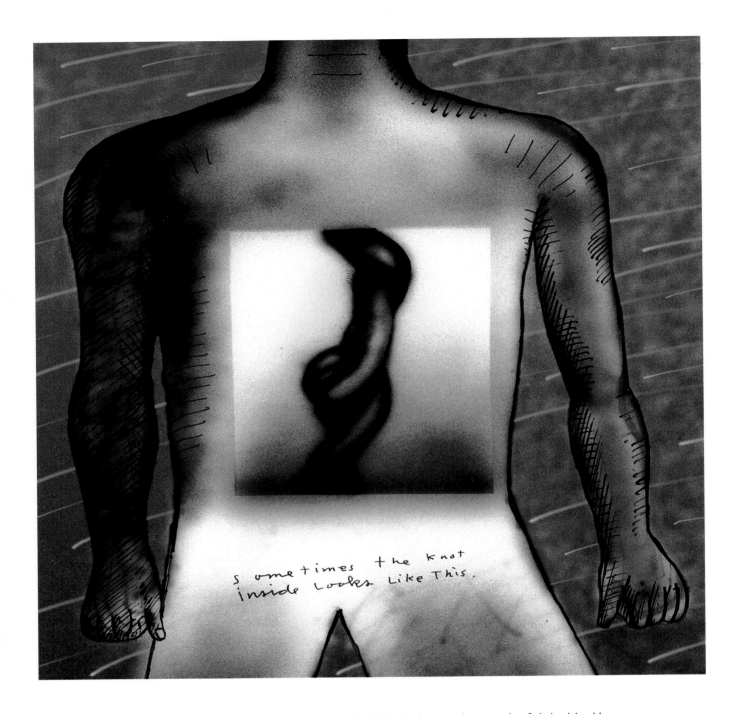

It was a strange day. He didn't know why. Maybe it was the way he felt inside. He was having a hard time putting his finger on it. Lots of FEAR. Lots of OUT OF CONTROL. He seemed to be going on a down cycle again. Wasn't it strange, he thought, how just a few days earlier he had known so much for sure, absolutely . . . how much real confidence he had had. But now something had turned, and that confidence was gone, vanished as if some unseen power had come along and decided he hadn't deserved it after all, and to teach him a lesson whisked it away to let him flounder awhile for his own good. As he stood there wondering how to stop the distinct feeling of getting smaller, his phone rang and for a split second he wondered whether to answer it or just let his machine take care of it as usual.

Man struggling with an
inability to properly express
himself in words.

(From a letter to Margaret)

. . . Someday I'm going to sit down and write all day to you. I can, you know, I never run out of things to say. It's going through my head all the time anyway, and the sooner my fingers learn to keep up with my thinking, the sooner I'm going to have some fun with the written word. What am I going to do without an electric typer in New Zealand? I'm afraid that little pixie thing I bought to travel with may not be too hot after all. It ain't got no speed, but I'll give it a chance and see what happens. Trouble is, my fingers are all geared up for electricity and speed, not thundering power, which is what it takes to get the keys on its left side to move, the ones I have to strike with my little finger. Maybe I can work my little finger out at the gym and put some good muscles on it before I come. Can you see me getting off the plane with this huge little finger?

"COME ONE, COME ALL, SEE THE WORLD'S MIGHTIEST LITTLE FINGER WORK INCREDIBLE WONDERS!"

In fact if all goes well and this finger does become something outstanding, I may have to have my visa changed from artist to showbiz personality.

"RICHARD, THE MAN WITH THE INCREDIBLE LITTLE FINGER!"

I could get a wheel for it and push it in front of me with chrome titles painted on its sides. In the long run I'd probably get jealous having to live in the shadow of a world-famous finger. And I wouldn't like that one bit. That is, until the fame receded and left the little but huge finger high and dry, something like what happened to Tiny Tim. I can't help wondering about people like that, where they go, what they do when their moment is over. I hope this never happens to me—Tiny Richard and his big little finger. Whatever happened to him, they'll say . . . or will they?

Yes Triumphs Over The Heartless No

Creativity is above all a mental act. Any time one has to make a choice, any choice, there is an opportunity to be creative and therefore the possibility to make more of one's life.

Craftsmanship and creativity are different things, relative but different. Creativity is much more important than craftsmanship in my opinion. Actually craftsmanship is just another tool for expressing what one chooses to express from the great caldron of possibilities. But someone's ability to craft something well does not make him or her an artist. I love and appreciate good craftsmanship, that's for sure, but it can be imitated and taught.

Creativity is another thing altogether. For me it is knowing myself enough to be aware of the distance between my aspirations and limitations, and then having the courage to create a life appropriate and uniquely my own—something that will nourish and sustain every action and thought, no matter what the rest of the world might do.

I don't hold that being an artist is either great or not great. Living is the art and what one produces should just be a part of that living—a reflection of the search for a better life.

Why crawl when you can walk. Why walk when you can run. Why run when you can Fly.

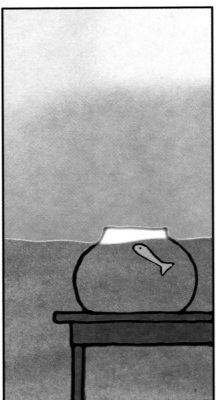

The FLOOD

We are most alive when we ~~attempt~~
~~to~~ do something, go somewhere,
accomplish something we thought impossible.
At that moment, that exhilarating moment,
there is only joy – blessed unadulterated JOY!
Fear has been conquered, at least for now.

It's about time:
  The time we have
  The Time we don't have.
      In The Relative world
Time measures the distance
between two points — how long
it takes to get from one to the other.

~~what if there are not~~
      what happens if we
by hook or crook eliminate
one of those two points?
  what then?
      ~~Does~~ time still exist?
      would

In a way time and space
  are the SAme. They both measure
~~a~~ a span of distance — They
both measure difference. They
both measure change.
  Space measures the distance
between 2 things.
      what if we eliminate the 2nd thing?
would space still exist?

Evolution Of An Enigmatic Expression

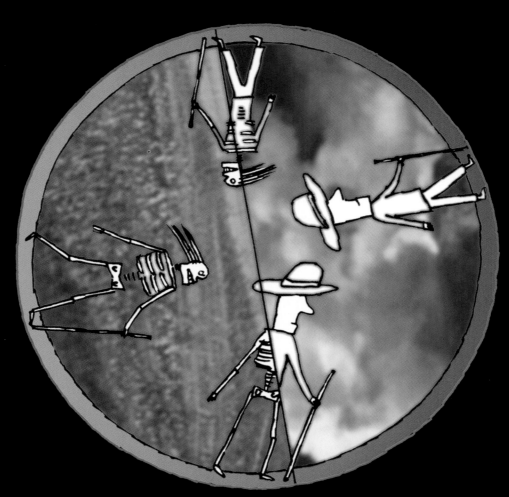

Sure

we only have
one life to live

but

how many births
and deaths
do will we have to experience
before we know
what that life
really is ?

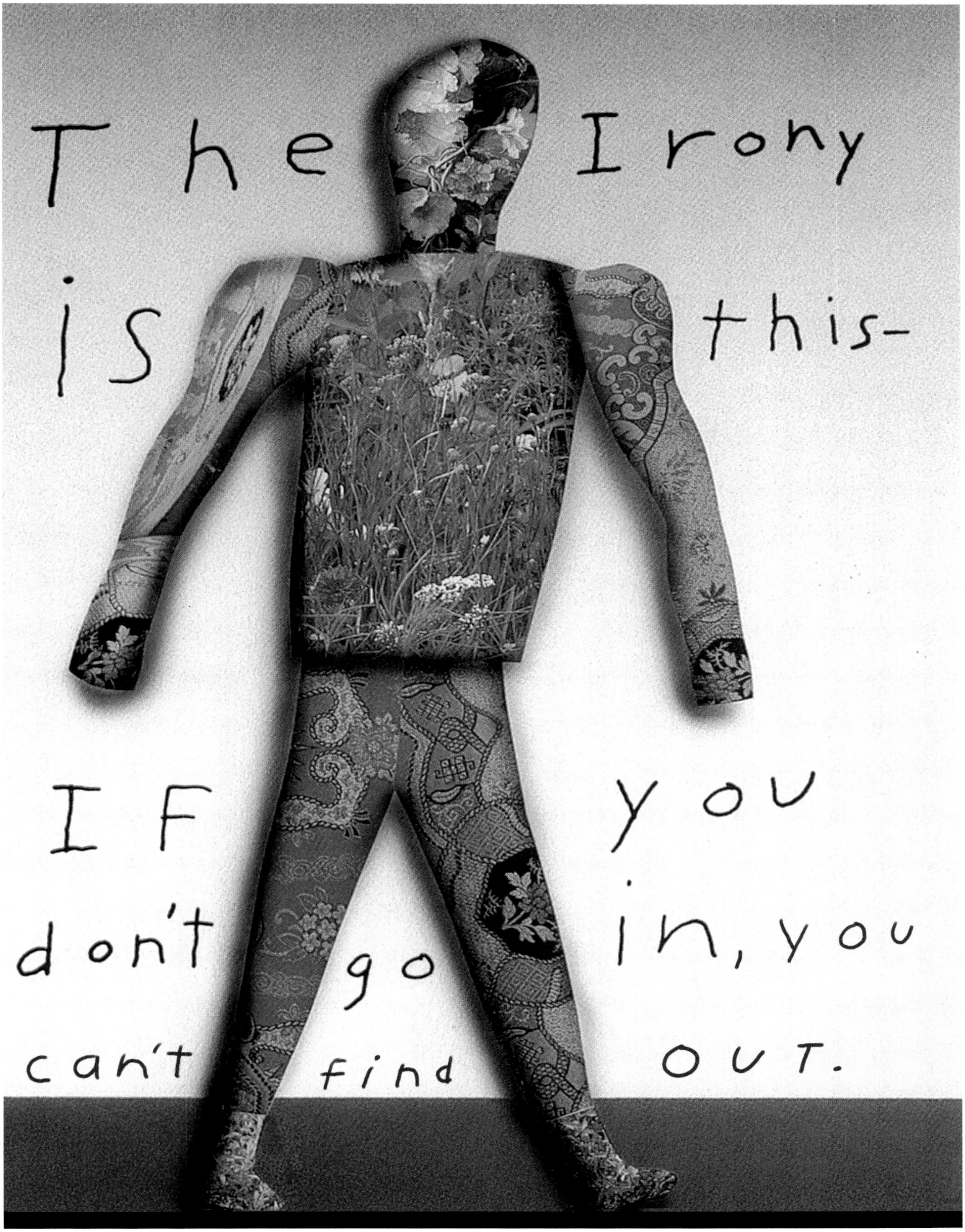

The Irony is this—

IF don't go you

can't find in, you

OUT.

THE HUNTER

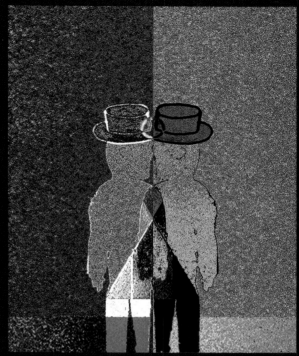

I SUSPECT THAT I HAVE NOT
FOUND WHAT I AM LOOKING FOR

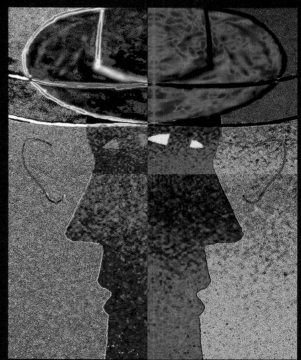

BECAUSE WHAT I NEED TO SEE
IS WHAT I AM LOOKING WITH.

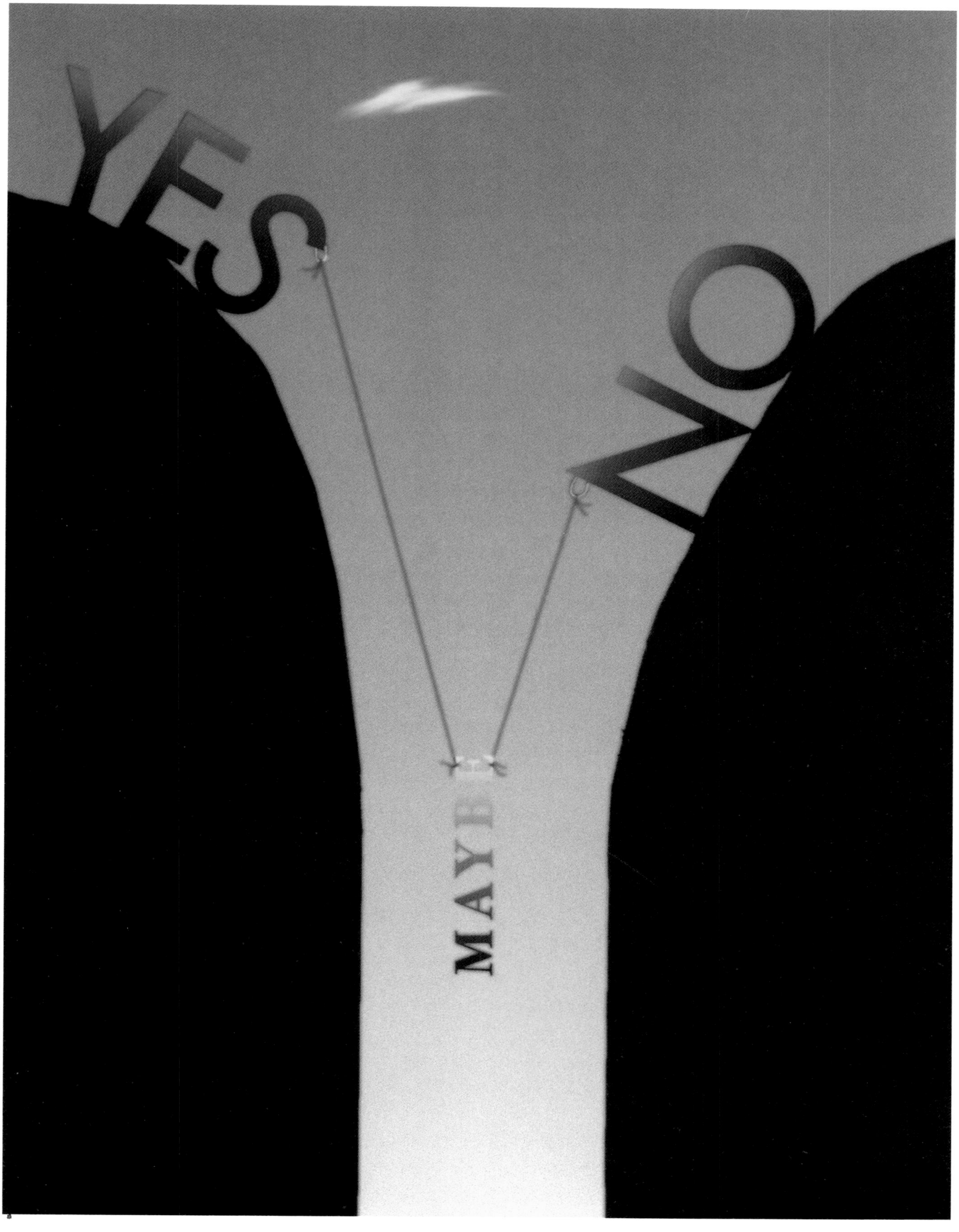

YES
NO
MAYBE

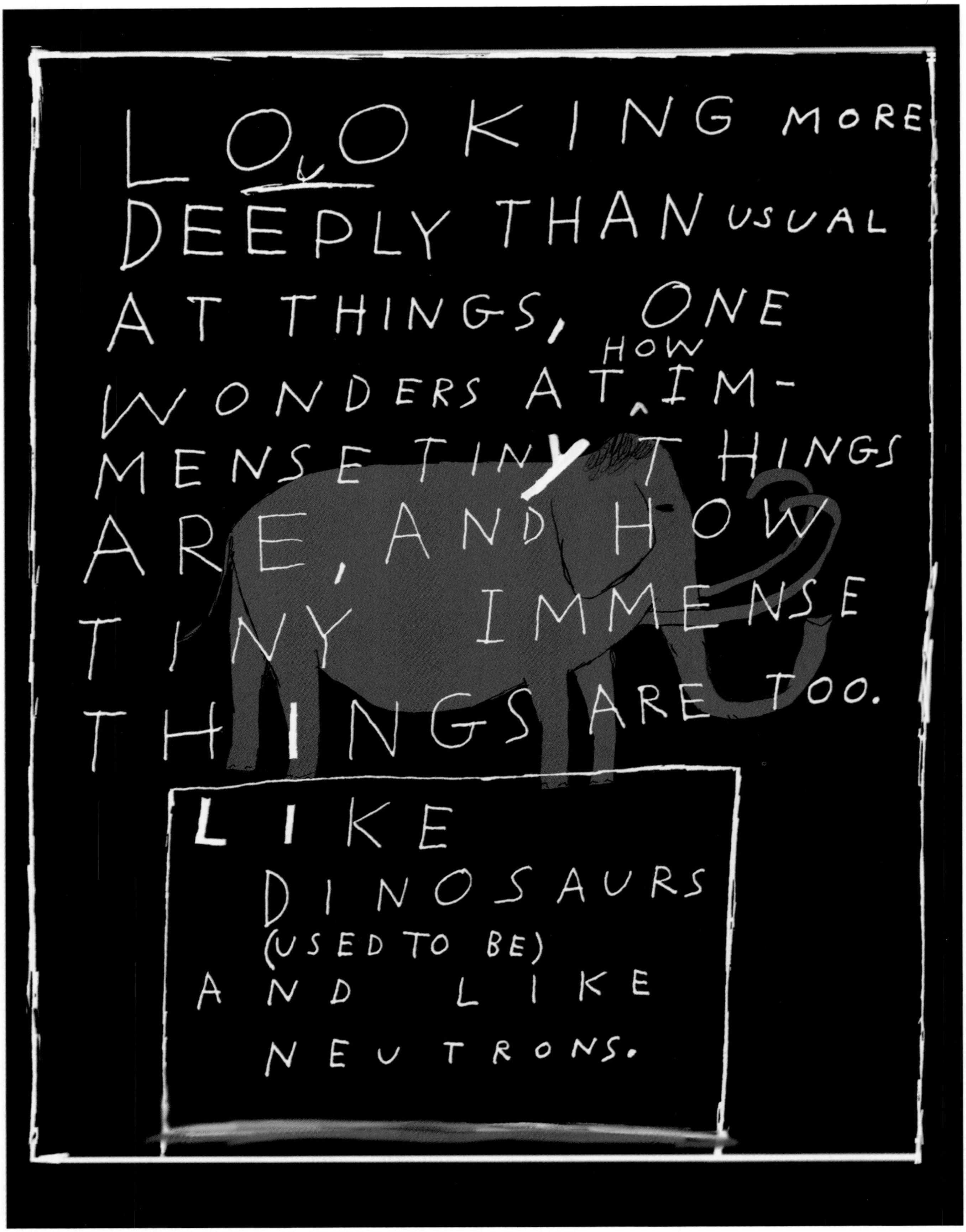

LOOKING MORE
DEEPLY THAN USUAL
AT THINGS, ONE
WONDERS AT, HOW IM-
MENSE TINY THINGS
ARE, AND HOW
TINY IMMENSE
THINGS ARE TOO.

LIKE
DINOSAURS
(USED TO BE)
AND LIKE
NEUTRONS.

It's about one's mind — how
it dictates the quality of
one's life — how it can go
up or down.

wanting the   mind to go up
is about try-   ing to aim
it toward   something
good, so   it can
be nur-   tured by
it and   grow.

It's hard to do sometimes,
especially if one feels
weak, or hurt, or angry.

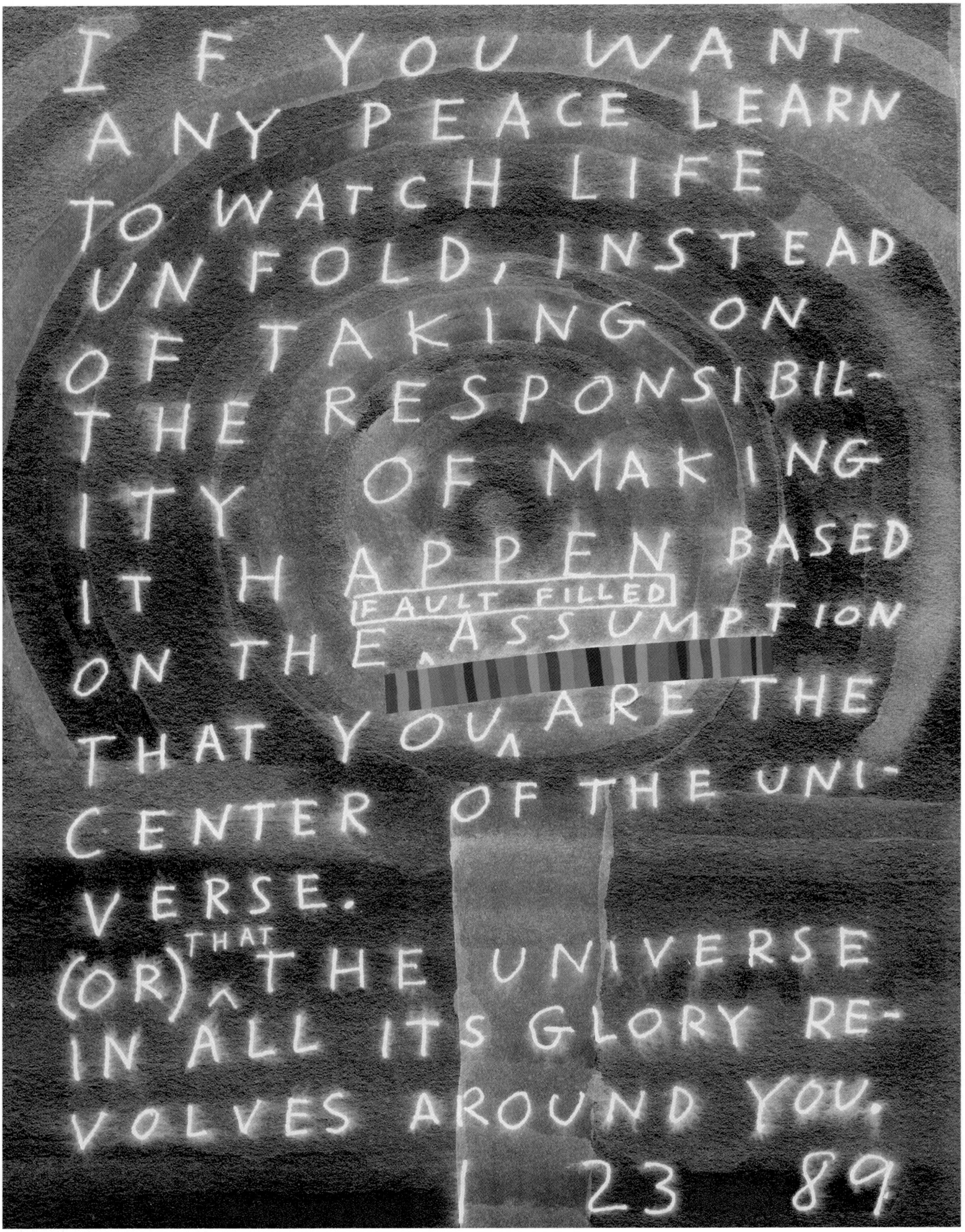

IF YOU WANT
ANY PEACE LEARN
TO WATCH LIFE
UNFOLD, INSTEAD
OF TAKING ON
THE RESPONSIBIL-
ITY OF MAKING
IT HAPPEN BASED
ON THE ASSUMPTION

FAULT FILLED

THAT YOU ARE THE
CENTER OF THE UNI-
VERSE.
(OR) THAT THE UNIVERSE
IN ALL ITS GLORY RE-
VOLVES AROUND YOU.
1 23 89

Hero's Bullet

What's the matter with having someone to look up to—a role model, a guide, a teacher?

What's the matter with watching someone who you believe has more intelligence and wisdom than you deal with the world, so you can learn how to deal better with it yourself?

What's the matter with being inspired by another human being?

Somehow, having a hero to learn from is looked on by some people as being a weakness. I see it otherwise. . . .

Woman Casting Her Image To The Wind

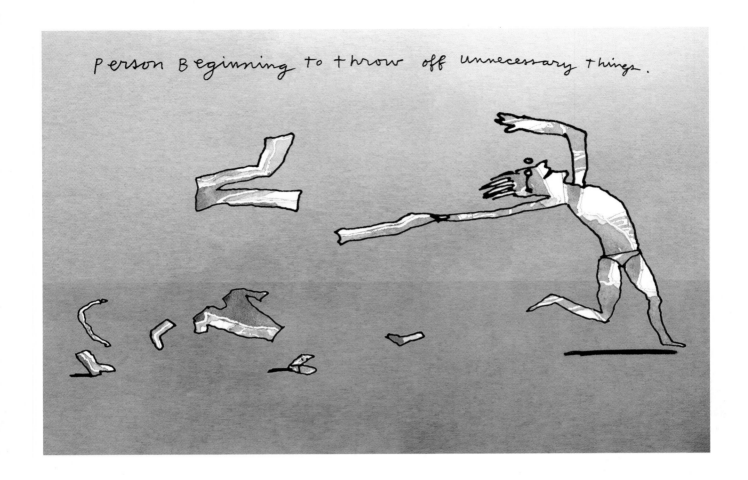

person Beginning to throw off unnecessary things.

Everything is always
in the process
of turning into
something else.

How many roads are there? As many roads as there are people

WE MOVED

NOT TOO LONG AGO WE SOLD almost EVERYTHING. WE HAD A MONSTER ART SALE, A MONSTER STUFF SALE, SOLD OUR HOUSE, AND GAVE EVERYTHING ELSE AWAY, AND MOVED. BEKINS BUT WE STILL HAD 33,000 lbs. OF THINGS TO HAUL.

WE HAD TO HOWEVER LEAVE OUR 7 POUND CAT BEHIND BECAUSE SINCE WE GOT THE BLACK DOG ABOUT A YEAR AGO SHE HAS BEEN LIVING ON THE ROOF WHICH IS FINE WHEN YOU LIVE IN SOUTHERN CALIFORNIA AND WHEN THE ROOF IS COVERED WITH WOOD SHINGLES AND SLANTS AT A NORMAL ANGLE → ← LIKE THIS, BUT WHEN YOU MOVE TO AN ISLAND IN THE NORTHWEST AND THE ROOF OF THE HOUSE YOU ARE GOING TO LIVE IN IS ALMOST ALL GLASS, AND IS VERY SLANTED, AND THE WINTERS ARE VERY WET AND COLD AND YOU STILL HAVE THE BLACK DOG THAT LOVES TO CHASE ANYTHING BUT MOST ESPECIALLY CATS THAT TRY TO RUN AWAY, THEN YOU'VE GOT TO FIND ANOTHER HOME FOR THE (OUR) CAT. WHICH WE DID. THEN, WHEN OUR 2 ESCROWS CLOSED WE LEFT HER THERE AND TOOK OFF WITH THE BLACK DOG. NOW WE ARE IN THE NEW HOUSE WITH THE GLASS ROOF THROUGH WHICH WE WATCH THE CLOUDS, STARS AND BIRDS FLY OVER AND THROUGH WHICH THE FULL MOON COMES IN O—WHICH IS BAD AND GOOD—BAD BECAUSE THE FULL MOON MAKES ME NERVOUS—GOOD BECAUSE IT MAKES INTERESTING SHADOWS AT NIGHT.

SOMETIMES I THINK ABOUT OUR 7 POUND CAT BACK IN SOUTHERN CALIFORNIA. I WONDER IF SHE LIVES ON THE ROOF OF HER NEW HOME AND I WONDER IF GOD HAS GIVEN HER ANOTHER BLACK DOG TO WORRY ABOUT. DO YOU BELIEVE IN GOD? I DON'T MEAN THE LITTLE TINY KIND, THE KIND WHERE YOU HAVE TO SQUEEZE YOURSELF INTO A BOOK WITH CHAPTERS THAT BLEED AND SAY THE RIGHT WORDS AND MEMORIZE, I MEAN THE BIG KIND, THE NO LIMITS, BEYOND WHAT IS BAD AND WHAT IS GOOD KIND. I DO. DON'T YOU JUST FEEL IT SO DEEP. LIKE HOW AFTER ALL COULD IT BE OTHERWISE?

Person Entering Another World At The Place Between Night and Day

There is no Beginning.
And there is no Ending.
Our experience is always
Only an excerpt.

Make no excuse for silence. It can speak for itself.

The father of a small boy was a pilot for a commercial airline. Often the boy's mother would take him to the airport to watch planes take off—something he did with awe and amazement.

One day the father decided he would give his son a thrill and took him aboard the big plane for his first flight. As soon as they had reached cruising altitude, the father went back to see his son and asked him how he'd liked the take-off. "Fine, Dad," the boy replied, somewhat hesitantly, "but when do we start to get smaller?"

Sometimes it's impossible to describe the places you've been and the things you've seen.

Not long ago I heard
what sounded like
an angel sing her
soft and lilting song
But
however hard I tried
I could not understand
her words,
and
what did it mean
when they gave her
a standing ovation
when it was over?
and
where did that
put me?

SEE INTO THE RIVER

Come, come to me. Sit here, rest awhile.
Maybe you would like to go with me a
ways. We can look at the clouds and
the sky and see joy and sorrow and
birth and death, and we can laugh
and cry together. Look up and down.
Both ways you will see into the
river, no banks, no bottom, deep
and constantly moving.

HOW to BUILD A FIRE

FIRST YOU CRUMPLE SOME NEWSPAPERS AND PUT THEM WHERE YOU WANT THE FIRE TO BE. NEWSPAPERS LIGHT EASILY AND BURN HOT. BUT NEWSPAPERS BURN FAST SO YOU NEED TO LAY SOME SMALL PIECES OF WOOD ON THE NEWS-PAPERS. WOOD BURNS SLOWER THAN THE NEWSPAPERS SO AFTER THE NEWSPAPERS HAVE BURNED THEY WILL HAVE SET THE SMALL PIECES OF WOOD ON FIRE. AND ONCE THE SMALL PIECES OF WOOD ARE BURNING YOU CAN ADD LARGER PIECES OF WOOD UNTIL THE FIRE IS GOING STRONG. Then YOU CAN PUT BIG LOGS ON THE small FIRE, AND AT LAST YOU WILL HAVE A BLAZE. THEN YOUR JOB OF BUILDING A FIRE WILL BE OVER AND YOU CAN SIT BACK AND RELAX AND ENJOY THE HEAT AND THE LIGHT.

Two Questions, Two Answers

Q.
How Long
do we have?

A.
As Long as
it takes.

Q.
How much
do we get?

A.
As much
as we need.

And so it goes...